Prepping: An Essential Guide for Every Prepper

The Survivalist Handbook for Doomsday Prepping

By: Marlon Chong

PUBLISHERS NOTES

Disclaimer

This publication is intended to provide helpful and informative material. It is not intended to diagnose, treat, cure, or prevent any health problem or condition, nor is intended to replace the advice of a physician. No action should be taken solely on the contents of this book. Always consult your physician or qualified health-care professional on any matters regarding your health and before adopting any suggestions in this book or drawing inferences from it.

The author and publisher specifically disclaim all responsibility for any liability, loss or risk, personal or otherwise, which is incurred as a consequence, directly or indirectly, from the use or application of any contents of this book.

Any and all product names referenced within this book are the trademarks of their respective owners. None of these owners have sponsored, authorized, endorsed, or approved this book.

Always read all information provided by the manufacturers' product labels before using their products. The author and publisher are not responsible for claims made by manufacturers.

Paperback Edition

Manufactured in the United States of America

DEDICATION

This book is dedicated to my family members and friends who have been very supportive of my endeavors throughout the years. The book is also dedicated to those persons who believe that the world as we know it is about to change and are making the necessary arrangements to ensure the safety and survival of themselves and their loved ones. I hope the information presented in this book will be as helpful to you, as it has been to me.

TABLE OF CONTENTS

CHAPTER 1- INTRODUCTION

Let's say a totalitarian government comes to power and starts building concentration camps. There are those who think that that's already underway on this continent. You see the handwriting on the wall, and in big bloody letters, and you decide it's time for you and your family to get out! Where would you go? How would you decide what the safest harbor would be? What criteria would you use to make that decision?

I have researched, for over 30 years, this particular subject. I've spent a ton of money in traveling all over the world and researching, but I think I'm just an ordinary person that had an epiphany some years ago that changed my life, the way that I look at things, and things started coming together. So, I don't have a PhD, I don't have a doctorate, but I'm a researcher and I've been involved in a lot of best-selling books and have put things together for people that have made a difference in their lives.

CHAPTER 2- AMERICA: A NATION ON THE BRINK OF CHAOS

Let's start with the tipping point, what could happen to make a move of this kind necessary? I want to give a little bit of a background here if I can about this. I think that there are two sides of this coin and, in all the people that I've talked to, it really has two sides. The United States, to me, already is too bad of a place to live in. Now, most people are going to think, "No, no, that's not the case," but I think we are the proverbial that sits in cold water, now it's boiling and we all think we're in a hot tub in Vegas, and everything is just peachy-keen and copasetic. I think there is massive deception in this country about how bad it already is. But yes, I think there's something that is going to be coming down the pike, and it's coming down the pike because of these years of research that I've done.

I've put the pieces of the puzzle together. I've looked and listened to the people that don't have an agenda, and I really do believe that there is a cabal group of persons, and I won't name names, but there are people out there that really can pull the strings. I think there are a lot of power hungry people that want to, but there is a group that is able to pull it off, and my greatest concern, right now, are these people, who because of their belief in eugenics want to reduce the world's population by 90%. They say it, they quote it, and they're not shy about it. So there are a lot of scenarios that can come down the pike.

If Obama wants to sign Martial Law into effect tomorrow, it can be done. It's just a signature, but there are a lot of things that could potentially happen; Another Chernobyl Fukushima type event, world war, look what's going on in the Middle East right now with Israel. Things could get out of hand. We know that there's going to be "tit for tat." There are countries that are raising their ugly heads against each other, they're fighting. Russia is threatening, China is threatening. Russia said, "Don't go into Syria," to the United States, and so the world powers are kind of at a very tense edge right now.

I think everybody knows that the economy of the United States is in deep problems. Anybody that lifts any grass knows that it wasn't too long ago we were the greatest credit nation on Earth. We had more money than everybody. Now, we're the greatest debtor nation on Earth. We have more debt than 90% of the countries in the world, combined.

The economy could collapse. We could get into hyperinflation. There could be a pandemic. We came close last year to potentially having one, where everybody has to be forced to be vaccinated. There are some people that just don't want to be vaccinated. We could have a natural disaster. Yellowstone could go. I really personally believe that there's going to be a lot of Earth changes that are going to be taking place, gravitational pulls and things. We're going to have greater earthquakes, greater weather anomalies and things like that. So there are a plethora of things that could possibly happen.

We are beyond the tipping point. I guess the tricky part would be deciding when to go. Now is the time to go. I believe it is, because of all of the people that I've already helped, that have already left the United States and expatriated out of the United States. I already know that there are millions of people who have left the country, because of taxation, and other things. But, probably, this is the other side of the coin that a lot of people don't look at. Do we have to wait until it's so bad that we don't want to live here anymore? Or, do we look at it that there is somewhere, or places on this planet that have a lot more freedom. They're tranquil, they're peaceful, they're real; they're just a better place to live.

For most persons, unless they're a Native American, or they're the descendant of a slave, their ancestors left the country of their birth and came to the United States. Now, not all of them came fleeing King George in England, or war or something absolutely horrible. Some of them just came for a better way of life.

The president could sign the country into Martial Law tomorrow. I happen to believe that there's going to be Debtor's Prisons, Concentration Camps, Re-education Centers, and all those sorts of things. These structures are now being built. What I tell people is this, "Stalin didn't build all those gulags to sit empty. Hitler didn't build all those concentration camps to sit empty. They were full to capacity." You don't spend that amount of time, energy and effort building these things and let them sit empty. I don't think it necessarily has to be we're at that stage where they're rounding people up. I constantly report to people that for every one person that left, or you can say "fled Europe" on the march of the Nazis all the way across Europe, 21 people stayed behind and died. Now, not everybody died in concentration camps. They could have died of starvation. They could have died by actually thinking they were going to amalgamate into the Nazi system. They joined the SS, the Gestapo, or whatever, thinking that they would rise to power and they would be okay in this system, and yet they died, either because they were sent to the frontlines, or because of the war itself. So I don't think that just going into the concentration camps is the only concern that we have here. I do think that they know (they, the people that will go nameless), they do know that the world is coming to an apex, that there's going to be an economic collapse.

We have rioting in the streets in Athens. We have rioting in the streets all over the world, in first world countries, in

Marlon Chong
civilized countries because of an economic crises, because of a lot of different things.

There's a breaking point for humanity, and we're seeing it all over the world, as countries are being overthrown. It's not just the Middle East, it's not North Africa.

CHAPTER 3- THE ILLUSION OF NATIONAL SECURITY

We have this mind-set in the United States, "It can't happen here". Oh, my! I really struggle with the people that think that it can't happen here. I think when it gets to a certain point it can happen. If a pandemic happens and people are forced-vaccinated, how many people do you know that are going to say "no" to the vaccine? There are people that are just itching for this thing to happen. Whether it's civil war or the collapse of civilization in the United States so they can take the country back. There are a lot of people that see this happening, they sense it's going to happen and I believe that it doesn't necessarily have to happen that way.

It could happen with Yellowstone, if Yellowstone goes, or some natural disaster, or some total economic collapse. Look at what's happening in Detroit with 30% or more unemployment. One hundred square miles of empty houses. The Mayor of Detroit wants to bulldoze 10,000, 15,000 or 20,000 homes because they're just completely vacated. When we have 20-30% unemployment in this country, we could have a big problem on our hands that the government will want to deal with in a way that we're going to freak out over.

One of the concerns that I think that most Americans should have is this: In the entire world, 7 billion people on the planet, there's about 9 million people in prisons. Twenty-five percent (25%) of those people are in the United States. The United States is 4.3% of the world's population, yet 25% of all the people in prisons are in the United States. That has never happened before, except in Stalinist Russia, Hitler's Europe, Pol Pot's Cambodia, etc. There should be some concern about this. All, you would think with those statistics, the highest incarceration rate in the world, 50% of all the countries in the world have one-tenth (1/10th) the amount of the incarceration rates the United States has. You'd think all of our criminals would be off the streets and they'd be in prisons. That's not so. The United States ranks as the highest crime country, and violent crime country in the world!

Now, there are three, four or five countries that have higher murder rates than we do. We're number one in the world in rape, and we're number two in the world in armed robbery. There is crime here. You can go places in the world where you don't have to worry about crime. If you worry about crime, it's like maybe having your stereo stolen out of your vehicle. Would you rather be raped, or would you rather have a stereo stolen out of your vehicle? Would you rather be murdered, or would you rather have your home burglarized? When it comes to violent crimes, Americans don't realize we're number one in the entire world. History is something we should learn from, or else it's going to repeat itself, and I'm just providing the statistics and the facts.

This whole thing that I've been doing is like doing a jigsaw puzzle. I'm putting pieces in and seeing the picture of the future, the future of the United States, the future of the world, based on all of the facts and the information that has been given to me. In the process of doing this, I began having these thoughts in my mind, "Well, this is probably going to happen and that's probably going to happen."

When those things did happen, as I saw the picture clearer, I didn't think of myself as a profit, in the way that people think of prophets today, like a religious prophet, or even Nostradamus Quatrains and all this stuff. I just thought, "Man, I'm putting things together, and I can see in to the future by just having a huge amount of information." I think that we can all look into the future by looking at all the pieces of the puzzle, putting as many in as we possibly can, and we can see the future. We really can see into the future.

CHAPTER 4- THE NEXT 5 TO 15 YEARS ON THIS PLANET

Most Americans may not want to think about it, but at the back of their minds they know that there's something innately wrong that's going on in the United States and in the world. What they don't want to have is no choices. Just like in Germany or all of Europe, there were rumours about what was going on. There were people going, "I'll never leave. I'll never leave my home, my family, etc." but there got to be a point in time where it got so bad that it was a choice of life and death. The people that waited too long, they got caught behind the lines.

I've spent 35 years doing this research, hundreds of thousands of dollars, travelled all over the world. I have put together a list of every country in the world, 200 countries in the world rated in 100 survival categories, and every country (from the best survival country in the world all the way to the 200th) is rated.

We all have some sort of insurance, whether it's insurance for our automobile just in case we're in a car accident, or we might have let's say candles and a flashlight in the house, just in case the electricity goes off, but it may never go off, but we still have them. We might have a gun in the house to protect our wife, children and daughter from being wrapped, or an intruder or something like that. We might have freeze-dried food, just in case martial law is called, or something goes bad at the grocery store. Well, this information is truly life and death. Maybe people would get this information and they would never use it; like buying a cookbook and never actually making any of the recipes. I think most people have done something like that, but this is the most important information when it comes to life and death, when it comes to surviving what I call the next 5 to 15 years on this planet.

You have a lot of shows on 2012 and a lot of things that are coming down in a prophetic sort of way. All of the world's religions, all of them, I've studied them in depth, have sort of what we'll call an "in time scenario," and almost all of them, have very similar bloodbaths and massive amounts of death on the planet. Scenarios before the Messiah returns or the Imam Mahdi, which is just in an uproar in Iran right now, or the Lord Maitreya and the 5th Buddha, Christ coming back, Jesus coming back, the Messiah coming back for the Jews. All of these scenarios are coming into play here, and there is the potential for war, the potential for disease epidemics, the potential for famine and starvation, and a huge amount of natural disasters, and ruthless government taking away our freedoms and our right to have, a high quality of life. This information gives people what they would know in the back of their minds, "I know where I'd need to go. I know why I'd want to go there."

I've researched so much. I really do believe that the United States has been targeted by the globalists to be taken out. They just have. As much as I love the United States and as much as I have a huge amount of feelings for the United States, we're right now the "big bully on the playground." We can kick into anybody's face. We can kick any of the kids off of the swing set, that are smaller than us, etc., but to have a global government, a new world order, to have the type of system they want in the world, you can't have one big huge bully going around, invading countries, assassinating people and killing people. You have to have this equal group of nations. I believe the United States is targeted, and I believe exactly that the people who do control the economies and global events in the world, have targeted the United States for destruction. I absolutely am convinced of it, and so I believe that you can hunker down here if you want to, and there will be a few people who will survive, but I believe 90% of the people in the United States that are alive today, that stay here, will be dead in the next 5 to 15 years.

Chapter 5 - The Safe Havens of the World

Some may ask "If there was a full-out nuclear war, Yellowstone blows, what difference does it make where you are? Those kinds of events are planetary, aren't they?" No, they are not. Let's take the planet that we live on and really do look at it. Let me give you some absolute, flat-out statistics. These are not opinions. This is absolute fact. Ninety percent (90%) of the world's population lives in the Northern Hemisphere. Ten percent (10%) of the world's population lives in the Southern Hemisphere. Ninety-five percent (95%) of all of the pollution generated in the world is generated in the Northern Hemisphere and does not cross the equator. That's called the cornealis effect. All the air and all the water, stays in its respective hemisphere. It does not cross the hemisphere. Think about it. Ten percent (10%) of the world's pollution is in the Southern Hemisphere, but it's half of the planet. Eighty-five percent (85%) of the world's rainforests that cleans the air and provides oxygen are in the Southern Hemisphere, and it only has to clean out 5% of the world's pollution. Climates in the Northern Hemisphere are much more severe than the Southern Hemisphere. In the Southern Hemisphere, global climate change doesn't change much of anything. Severe changes in the Northern Hemisphere.

There are so many people in the Northern Hemisphere, there are tensions, war, there's fighting over the few resources. It is completely different; in the Southern Hemisphere, it is quiet, tranquil, and peaceful.

I've been a few places in Southern Africa. It is a completely different way of life. If you have another Fukushima, or you have a nuclear war, all that, is going to generate in the Northern Hemisphere. None of that radiation, those isotopes, the iodine-131, the uranium, plutonium or stramonium, crosses the equator and goes to the Southern Hemisphere. So if there's nuclear war between the United States and China, the United States and Russia, or Pakistan, and things start getting out of hand, Pakistan, India or whatever, all of that's going to circulate in the Northern Hemisphere.

The whole bottom part of the southern part of South America, which would be Uruguay, Chile and Argentina, are in the top five of the countries for survivability, but there's more to it than just the Southern Hemisphere. I mean, there are these one hundred categories of survivability. I have ranked the countries based on various factors but I think it would be a disservice if I said, "Go to country A, B, C," and I'll tell you why. To me, and I've heard this from a lot of people, it would be like getting one of those bookcases or some piece of furniture that you have to kind of put together and didn't have instructions.

I have this "best of" and "worst of" series. If you're really into one particular subject – let's say, you're scared of being bitten by a mosquito and dying of malaria. Well, I put all those countries in there that have diseases like malaria, etc. If you have the most money, or you have very little money and you want the best "bang for your buck," I give you the poor countries that have survivability where you can go and live a very good quality of life. I list all these different things and give you the ability to choose, based upon your personal choice, but they're safe against what I call "the five big killers," which are war, disease, famine, starvation, natural disasters, and as I call it "ruthless government." I believe that, of all the deaths that are going to take place in the next 5 to 15 years, it's going to be because of these five things: war, disease, famine, natural disasters and ruthless government.

There are places where I'm predicting 4% of that population will die, but the vast majority of the countries are going to survive. I believe, in this collapse of civilization and with war and all of the other things that are going to take place.

Immigration Polices

Some persons often ask. "Will those countries let us in will the United States let us out?" There are some countries that are easier to get into than others. There are still a few countries that are not so overwhelmed in their immigration offices by Americans and Europeans, but let me tell you, millions of Europeans and millions of Americans are moving to these countries, and they are overwhelming the immigration offices. So they are going to make it more difficult, as the day goes by, as every week goes by, to be able to have Americans get in.

Ecuador, I've just recently helped a family move to Ecuador with five kids. It's an incredible place. It's a lot of people that are moving to Ecuador for various reasons now. It's directly on the Equator. It is in the top five, but all the countries are in the Southern Hemisphere, and well almost all of them are in the top 20. There are a few countries that are in the Northern Hemisphere, but it's difficult to get into some countries. Look at Australia and New Zealand. You have to have a lot of money. You have to speak English. You have to be young, yet you have to have spent your whole career in the same business.

It's a point system, and I give the details about getting into certain countries, and how difficult it is, or how easy it is. There's no easy country to move into. If you and I owned a country, would we just let anybody in? No, of course not. Would we let all the criminals in? No, of course not. We'd want educated people, people that aren't going to leech off of the government, etc. So there are things that you have to do, but I've done it. I've helped many people do it. It's not that difficult. If you have a will to do it, it can be done.

The worst thing that could ever happen to any human being is regret. You don't want any regrets, especially when it comes to your family. You want to do what's right by them; you want to have options. You want to live. You want to live a high quality of life. I think that most people know that something is going on in the world, and especially in this country, that just isn't right.

The Cost of Migrating

For an average family, for somebody of normal means, or less than normal means, that is a daunting task to be able to afford to move your family, sell all your possessions, decide what you're going to take with you and then leave the country on the assumption that things are really going to get bad in a big hurry, and it is also under the assumption that you can do this and get out in time. These are all noted considerations. But the bottom line is there are people looking for a better life now. So even if it doesn't hit the fan, you don't have to wait until, you know, the worst case scenario or whatever is happening, or death is knocking on the door, like we did in Europe and the Nazis on the march. We could look at this as, "Why are the millions of people that are leaving every year leaving?" They're leaving for a lot of different reasons. Some do see the handwriting on the wall, but other people are looking for a better way of life. People have moved from LA to Chicago or from San Francisco to Miami. It's a move. There's a cost involved in moving, certainly. There is some paperwork that you have to get to, to get into any country. They're just not going to let anybody in, but it's for a better way of life. It's not the easiest thing in the world to do, but what's the alternative? Do you want to live in a country where you are trapped and traced and you could lose it all right now? You could lose everything you've got right now because we live in the most litigious society in the world! Somebody could sue you and I don't care how much insurance that you have, just you paying attorneys could bleed you dry. We live in a society in this country where you could lose it all one hundred different ways. You could even loose it due to sickness. The vast majority of bankruptcies, way over 50% of all bankruptcies are due to medical bills, and those are with people with medical insurance. So how would you like to live some place where everything is healthy and organic and people live a longer life?

All the major world globalists, such as Ted Turner who says population of the planet, should be no more than 500 million people, own land in the Southern Hemisphere. Ted Turner owns tons of land in the southern part of South America. George Soros, who can make one statement and ruin a country, ruin an economy; there are very few people as powerful as he is, and he owns tons of land in this area of southern South America as well. The vast majority of the globalists have safe havens in the safe havens. They know what's going on. They know what's coming down. Now, Russia, the United States and a few other countries have a lot of underground cities where they're going to take their political leaders when we have nuclear, or let's say Planet X ibiru, the Brown star, and I mean there are many scenarios out there that are coming down the pike. It could be that just some people within governments know, but it's not widely shared. I think that there are some people within the United States Government who run the show, but I think the vast majority of the people in the United States government are not aware. It's kind of hush-hush in certain circles, and in other circles, they are planning and preparing for this. You know, look at the tsunamis that we've had. I tell you what, if we have a polar flip and the ice melts at both poles, if we have some major disasters in some ways, if the seas rise 20 feet, one billion people are going to be displaced. That's one out of every seven people on the planet. There are some things that are going down, they know the scenarios, and they're preparing for themselves. They're not preparing for you or me. I believe that we are probably one of the least free countries in the world and yet we're touted to be one of the most free. I think they just keep us here to support this government.

Left Wing or Right Wing?

Some persons have asked "But doesn't some of the countries on your list such as Chile, have Leftist Leadership? I do not believe in the Left-Right paradigm. I believe in freedom and whether you are Left or you're Right, whether you're a Republican or a Democrat, if you're black or white, rich or poor, if you're a Catholic, Protestant, atheist, metaphysical or whatever it is, you would want to live in a Libertarian society where nobody hates you. Yes, there has been Left and Right politicians in all of these countries in South America, as well as South Africa. There has been extreme Left and extreme Right, and the same thing that's going on in Europe and various other places.

I think you have to look at survival. Chile is not that Libertarian. Chile has some problems and issues with it. I mean, they have a lot of earthquakes, they have volcanoes, and they have some issues like natural disasters. Granted, I'm predicting only 10% of the people that die in the world will die of natural disasters, but that's still 10%. That's one bullet in a ten-chamber revolver playing Russian roulette. I think there are places that you have to look at totally. If you don't think that there are going to be any earth changes, etc., then that's not a problem. As I mentioned, some of the big shots have bought up a bunch of land in places such as Paraguay, even though it's a military dictatorship. I guess if you've got friends who run the military dictatorship, that's probably a good place to be. Paraguay is a military dictatorship. Uruguay is not, Argentina is not, Chile is not, Ecuador is not and Brazil is not. Most of the southern parts, southern countries do not have military dictatorships, but Paraguay certainly does

As it related to retiring in one of these countries, I have immigration information on all the top countries, the survival countries and what the immigration rules and regulations are. There are various different ways to get into some countries. Ecuador, by the way, is one of the easiest countries to get into right now that's in my top five, but there are countries that are more difficult, but it depends on your age, it depends on your finances. There are a lot of variables there.

Chapter 6- Nations with a Higher Standard of Living

Most of all the countries in South America have a higher standard of living than the United States. In the United States, the vast majority of people are in debt up to their eyeballs. In other countries such as those found in South America, most people own their homes. The country in which I live, less than 3% of all the homes in the whole entire country have a mortgage on them. That means when you buy a home you pay cash for it. You pay cash for everything. So for all those people concerned about those economic issues know, from a Christian point of view, people say "mark of the beast," or those tracking and tracing, RFID sort of things, that is not going to be the problem that it is going to be in most of the other countries in the world. Brazil, Argentina, all these countries have pros and cons. They all have their different economic things, but let's say for example for Argentina, all the charts are going up, economically speaking, and the charts for the United States are all going down. The United States has almost twice the unemployment that Argentina has. So the economic indicators are completely different. Most of these countries that are in our top five, top ten, their economies are really moving forward. There's a lot of investment. There are millions of people that are leaving. They are going to these countries because you have a higher quality of life.

The globalists have said it. All the world's religions predict these sorts of things. It's all coming down, and if you want to stick it out, and you want to fight for this country, you can. But, your relatives, your ancestors left the country of their birth and came to the United States looking for a better live, or fleeing certain death or destruction. You can't say that the people that are leaving the United States are not intelligent, or they're not doing the right thing for themselves. It's not for everybody, but you go ahead, you stick it out here and you see what happens. This is the façade that we have here. You're in Vegas, George, good grief! You know what's happened to the housing market there; 25% of every home in the United States, people owe more on it than what they could get if they sold it today. They don't own that home. The bank does. The bank owns their cars, and because of their credit card debt, if they sold everything they had, they would end up with either a negative, or very, very little, maybe the clothes on their back. In these other countries, everybody owns their home. They own their car. If economic things happen, nothing changes!

Marlon Chong

They grow their food in their backyard. They're self-sufficient. It's not going to be as devastating as the people here in this country that will have absolutely nothing when the economy collapses. Millions of people are fleeing the United States. Millions have already left. According to the Zogby poll, tens of millions are planning to leave, shortly. They're already making plans. So, certainly, if you don't think that you can do it, you can.

Anyone can Google Frances Fox Piven, or Cloward and Piven. These are two Socialists who are working with the DSA, the Democratic Socialists of America, to create chaos and bring down Capitalism. They're out there today. If you look at a picture of when President Clinton signed the Motor Voter Bill, standing behind him are none other than Cloward and Piven.

As it relates to re-education camps, is there are YouTube videos. An FBI agent infiltrated the weatherman associated with Obama's friend, Bill Ayers, when he headed up the weatherman and the SDS, (Students for Democratic Society), and in this meeting, they openly discussed re-education camps being created down in Georgia, upon the collapse and the chaos, once they were able to collapse the economy. They were going to send Americans to the re-education camps, and they were discussing what they were going to do to those who were unwilling to become re-educated. They estimated that they would have to murder 25 million Americans who would not succumb to their re-education. These are facts, and they're chilling, and people better wake up because there are people in America who are plotting, peoples like George Soros, to collapse our country's economy, our civil society and our way of life, and although there are a lot of NRA members, who will stand up and fight along with our military, it may not be enough if there's total economic collapse.

Overall, I think people have their perception of things. I am a truth seeker. I want all the information that I can possibly grab, and put all of these pieces of the puzzle together. When you start putting the pieces of the puzzle together, you're going to see the handwriting on the wall in this country, and you're going to want at least an option, and that's what I give people. I give people information on how and where to survive the collapse, whether it's nuclear war, whether it's disease and pandemics, whether it's famine, starvation or hyperinflation, economic disaster or ruthless governments, whether it's a Fascist Right-wing Hitler-type takeover, or a

Communist Stalinist takeover of this country, or a military dictatorship, if it's natural disasters, global climate change, whatever, there's places that you can go that are going to survive.

The statistics don't lie. I've travelled these countries. I've investigated them and what can I say? The people that have done it just tell me incredible information, life-saving information. The people that have actually left the country say that it's the best thing that they've ever done.

The American Government is preparing for something and they create these laws in order to control more American people. I still believe the average American does not know that they're the frogs in cold water; they think that they're okay, and they are now boiling. It's boiling. They think there in a hot tub in Vegas. They're not. The massive deception is there. They're going to be dinner here shortly. I mean I'm not going to pick on the United States government, per se, but I think that they are prepared. I mean, I've seen and I think most people have seen the pictures of the millions of coffins they have ready, the body bags

Lower Cost of Living

As far as a home, 15 years ago, you could have bought a brand new, three-bedroom, two-bath really nice home for probably about $20,000, US dollars, where I live. I live in an ex-pat area, very, very first world high quality sort of an area. You just have no idea what it's like to buy tomatoes for 10 cents/pound and come back to the United States and buy them for $2/pound. There are a lot of variables that are going on. There's inflation, there are a lot of things that are changing economies in countries and stuff. You can look at each individual country and what the cost of things are. Certainly, if you went to Switzerland, if you went to Norway, if you went to Italy, you're going to pay more than you do in the United States, but there are countries where you can get the best value for your money.

The Unbelievers

Many people argue that America was founded by Protestants running away from Catholic countries and in 1776 when they finally put it together they had a 10-to-1 majority over the Catholics, and 55 of the 56 signers of the Declaration of Independence were Protestants. Today, we have half our 300 million populations are Protestants. You brought 50 people into the area where you live as Americans, down in South America. You're talking to 10 million people tonight. There's 150 million Protestants who are still here who can turn this situation around.

I like living as a Libertarian where you can be a Protestant, a Catholic, or a New-Ager. You can believe in anything and nobody is going to harm you. Nobody cares because they're Libertarian. They're in a completely different mind-set.

Recommendation

They think they're going to take back the country and with the 140 million Protestants, I don't get it, but anyway I wish them well. Relocating may seem daunting. I think that's a misnomer. I mean, have you ever gotten on a plane and gone to LA, New York, or Toronto? Have you gone to the Caribbean? Have you gone to Hawaii? It's no different. You just go, and you take a week or two vacation and investigate. Do your due diligence and go, "Wow, this sounds like the country for me." Best of all, the countries are very close together, unless you want to go to Australia, New Zealand or someplace else. You can investigate. But I give the one, two, three, the ABCs of what to do, of how to investigate the websites. There are hundreds of blogs, hundreds of websites, hundreds of bits of information about any particular country that you want. It's there on the internet to investigate.

ABOUT THE AUTHOR

Marlon Chong is a published author who has spent decades researching the landscape, economy, politics and culture of many of the world's nations. The author has spent a significant portion of his career using the findings of his research to determine the likelihood of a collapse of the U.S economy. He also uses this information to help persons to prepare themselves and increase their chances of survival in the event of such a crisis.

In this book the author provides information on the more favorable cost of living and overall improved standard of living to be experienced in other regions of the world that are projected to be less affected by the impending events.